<u>Dedication</u>

I would like to thank my friends and my wife for their continued support. I hope this book truly makes your life better and easier.

This book was written by Daniel Melehi with the A.I assistance of Inventabot.com

Daniel Melehi

Contents

2

3

Chapter 1: Understanding Macros. Macros are powerful tools in Excel that can help automate repetitive tasks, reducing errors and increasing efficiency. In this chapter, we will explore what macros are, the benefits of using them, and macro security.

SUBCHAPTER 1.1: WHAT ARE MACROS?

Simply put, macros are recordings of actions you take in Excel that can be played back at a later time. They are made up of a series of instructions that can automate tasks and save time by reducing the need for manual input. For example, a macro can be created to sort and filter data, create graphs, or perform calculations.

SUBCHAPTER 1.2: BENEFITS OF USING MACROS

There are numerous benefits to using macros in Excel. First and foremost, macros can help save time and reduce errors by automating repetitive tasks. This allows users to focus on more high-level work, such as data analysis. Additionally, macros can help standardize processes and tasks across teams, ensuring consistency and accuracy.

SUBCHAPTER 1.3: MACRO SECURITY

While macros can be incredibly useful, they can also pose a security risk if not properly managed. Malicious code can be hidden within macros, and when they are executed, they can potentially modify or steal data on the user's computer. Excel has several security features to help protect users from these risks, including enabling or disabling macros, digital signatures, and password protection. It is important to understand and properly utilize these security features to ensure the safe use of macros in Excel.

Chapter 1: Understanding Macros

In this chapter, we will explore the world of macros.

SUBCHAPTER 1.1: WHAT ARE MACROS?

Macros are essentially shortcuts, which automate repetitive tasks in Excel. With the help of macros, you can perform a series of actions with just a click of a button. In Excel, a macro is a set of instructions that are recorded in VBA (Visual Basic for Applications) and can be executed manually or automatically. Macros can be used to perform simple tasks like formatting cells, inserting formulas, or carrying out complex tasks like performing data analysis, consolidation, and reporting.

SUBCHAPTER 1.2: BENEFITS OF USING MACROS

The use of macros can greatly streamline your workflow in Excel and increase your productivity. Here are some benefits of using macros:

Automation of Repetitive Tasks

Macros can automate repetitive tasks, saving you time and effort while eliminating errors that arise from manual operations.

Efficient Handling of Large Data Sets

Macros can help in analyzing and reporting on large data sets by performing calculations or data consolidation tasks that can take a lot of time to handle manually.

Consistent Actions

By standardizing procedures with macros, you can ensure that all actions are performed consistently across your organization, regardless of who is doing the task.

SUBCHAPTER 1.3: MACRO SECURITY

Macros can potentially pose a security risk. As macros are a form of executable code, they can contain malicious content. It is vital to evaluate the source of any macros, and only enable macros from trusted sources. To reduce risks it is important to be aware of macro security settings such as disabling all macros, enabling all macros, or only enabling macros from trusted sources. Overall, it is important to ensure that proper macro security protocols are set up in Excel.

WHAT ARE MACROS?

Macros are a series of commands and instructions that are stored in Visual Basic for Applications (VBA) which can be used to automate repetitive tasks in Excel. Macros allow you to perform a series of complex actions with just a simple click of a button. The beauty of macros is that they are time-saving tools that can help you speed up your work, avoid manual errors and increase efficiency. To put it simply, macros allow you to record a set of actions and then replay them whenever you need to. Whether it's formatting data, applying formulas, or creating charts, macros can carry out tasks with precision and accuracy, enabling you to focus on more important aspects of your work. In short, macros are a powerful tool that everyone who works with Excel should know how to use. In the next subchapter, we will delve deeper into the benefits of using macros.

BENEFITS OF USING MACROS

Macros can greatly improve your efficiency and productivity when working with Excel. Here are some of the key benefits of using macros:

1. Time Savings

One of the biggest advantages of using macros is the time savings it provides. Recording and running a macro can perform repetitive tasks in seconds, which would have taken hours if done manually. For example, if you need to format a report with a specific font, size, and color, you can record a macro that applies those changes to the entire document with a single click, saving you hours of time.

2. Accuracy

Macros can help you to reduce errors and improve accuracy. Unlike humans, macros don't get tired, bored, or distracted, which means they can consistently perform a task with the same level of accuracy, every single time. This minimizes the risk of mistakes being made and saves time on fixing them.

3. Consistency

Macros can help enforce consistency in tasks that require the same steps to be performed repeatedly. With a recorded macro, you can ensure that each task is completed using the same settings, every time it is executed.

4. Customization

Excel macros can be customized to suit your specific needs. You can record a macro that performs a task in a particular way, and then modify the code to add new features or tweaks. This means that you can tailor each macro to suit your specific requirements, which can save significant time and increase accuracy in your work.

5. Enhanced Functionality

Macros can expand the range of tasks that you can perform in Excel. They can automate complex tasks such as data entry, report generation, and analysis, and even interact with other applications such as Outlook, Word, and Access. With macros, you can create powerful and sophisticated workflows that would be impossible to achieve with manual tasks alone. Overall, the benefits of using macros in Excel are clear. They save time, reduce errors, and increase consistency and accuracy of tasks. In the next chapter, we'll learn how to record macros in Excel.

MACRO SECURITY

As powerful as macros can be for automating repetitive tasks and streamlining workflows, they can also introduce potential security risks if not properly managed. Macro malware has been a persistent threat in the cybersecurity landscape, and Excel macros are a common vector for this type of attack. To safeguard against malicious macros, it is important to understand the security options available in Excel. Microsoft provides various settings and features that allow you to control macro behavior and minimize risk. One of the most basic and effective steps you can take is to ensure that your copy of Excel is always up to date with the latest security patches and updates. Additionally, Excel has a security feature that disables macros by default, called Macro Security. It's recommended that you leave this feature enabled to prevent unauthorized code execution. Macro Security settings can be accessed through the Excel Options menu. Here you can choose between four security levels, ranging from "Disable all macros without notification" to "Enable all macros". The safest option is to set it to "Disable all macros with notification", which prompts you to enable macros whenever a file containing them is opened. You may also choose to digitally sign your macros to ensure that they are trusted and not corrupted. This can be done through the Visual Basic Editor, where you can generate a digital signature for your macros and a certificate to verify their authenticity. By following these basic security practices, you can enjoy the benefits of Excel macros without sacrificing the safety of your data and systems.

Chapter 2: Recording Macros

When it comes to working with Excel, time is of the essence. Recording macros can save you a significant amount of time and can streamline your workflow.

SUBCHAPTER 2.1: STEPS TO RECORD A MACRO

Recording a macro is a simple process that can be done in a few steps. Firstly, navigate to the "Developer" tab in the ribbon menu and click on "Record Macro". Give your macro a name and choose the location where you want to save the macro. Now you can start recording the actions you wish to automate. All the actions you perform while recording the macro, such as formatting data or entering values, will be recorded and saved in the macro code. Once you have completed all the actions, you can stop recording the macro by clicking on "Stop Recording".

SUBCHAPTER 2.2: EDITING AND DEBUGGING MACROS

Once you have recorded a macro, you may need to edit or debug it. This is especially true if the recorded macro is not achieving the intended result. You can edit a macro code by navigating to the "Developer" tab and clicking on "Visual Basic". This will open the Visual Basic Editor, where you can modify the macro code. When debugging a macro, you can use the "Step Into" and "Step Over" buttons to go through the code line by line and identify any errors or bugs.

SUBCHAPTER 2.3: BEST PRACTICES FOR CREATING MACROS

When recording macros, it's important to follow best practices to ensure your code is efficient and effective. Some best practices include keeping your macro code concise and well-organized, using meaningful names for variables and macros, commenting your code to make it easier to understand, and testing your macro thoroughly before using it in your workflow. Additionally, avoid using absolute references in your macro code, and instead, use relative references to ensure your macro works regardless of the location of your data.

STEPS TO RECORD A MACRO

Recording a macro is an easy way to automate repetitive tasks in Excel. Here are the steps to record a macro: 1. Open the workbook and navigate to the "Developer" tab in the ribbon. If you don't see the "Developer" tab, you may need to enable it in Excel's options. 2. Click on the "Record Macro" button in the "Code" section of the ribbon. 3. In the "Record Macro" dialog box, specify a name for your macro and choose a shortcut key to assign to it. You can also add a description for your macro to help you remember what it does later. 4. Choose where you want to store the macro. You can either store it in the current workbook or in your personal macro workbook if you want to use it across multiple workbooks. 5. Click "OK" to start recording your macro. 6. Perform the actions you want to automate. This could include formatting cells, entering data, or any other task you want to automate. 7. When you're finished, click on the "Stop Recording" button in the "Code" section of the ribbon. That's it! Your macro is now ready to use. You can trigger it by pressing the shortcut key you assigned to it or by selecting it from the "Macros" button on the

"Developer" tab. But before you start using your macro, it's important to test it to make sure it works as intended.

CHAPTER 2: RECORDING MACROS

Subchapter 2.2: Editing and Debugging Macros

After successfully recording a macro, you may need to modify it to suit your needs. This involves editing the recorded code to add or remove actions or to change their parameters. This is done in the VBA (Visual Basic for Applications) editor. To open the VBA editor, press **Alt + F11** or go to the Developer Tab and click *Visual Basic*. This will open a new window displaying the code for the current workbook. From here, you can select the module containing the macro you want to edit and make the necessary changes. Once you have made changes, you can test the macro by running it again from the Macros dialog box. However, errors may occur when running macros, either due to changes in the workbook or due to mistakes in the code. In such cases, you can use the debugging feature of the VBA editor. To debug a macro, you can set breakpoints in the code by clicking on the line where you want to pause execution and pressing **F9**, or by selecting the line and going to *Debug > Toggle Breakpoint.* Then, run the macro as usual. The code will stop executing at the breakpoint, allowing you to inspect variables and step through the code one line at a time using the **F8** key. This can help you identify and correct any errors in the code. Remember to always test your macros thoroughly before using them in a production environment. Additionally, make sure to follow best practices for creating macros to ensure that your code is efficient and reliable.

BEST PRACTICES FOR CREATING MACROS

When creating macros, there are certain best practices you should follow to ensure that your code is efficient, effective and easy to maintain. These practices include:

1. Keep it Simple:

When writing macros, it's best to keep your code as simple as possible. This means avoiding unnecessary loops, conditions and other complex programming structures. The simpler your macro, the easier it will be to understand and maintain.

2. Comment Your Code:

It's important to comment your code as you write it. This will help you and others understand what your macro does and how it does it. Use clear and concise comments to explain each step of your code.

3. Use Meaningful Names:

When naming your macros, use meaningful names that describe what the macro does. Avoid using abbreviations or cryptic names that might confuse others who are trying to understand your code.

4. Test Your Macros:

Before you put your macros into production, make sure to test them thoroughly. This means running the macro on a sample data set to make sure it produces the desired results. You should also test your macro on different versions of Excel to ensure that it will work on all platforms.

5. Keep Security in Mind:

When creating macros, it's important to keep security in mind. Excel macros can be a security risk if they are not written carefully. Always use macro security settings to restrict the use of macros to trusted sources.

6. Organize Your Macros:

It's important to organize your macros in a logical manner to make them easy to find and use. You can do this by creating a macro library, grouping similar macros together, and using naming conventions to identify related macros. By following these best practices, you can create macros that are efficient, effective and easy to maintain. With a little planning and attention to detail, you can turn Excel macros into a powerful tool for automating your workflow.

Chapter 3: Modifying Macros

EDITING MACROS

Macros can be modified to fit changing needs in your workflow. Editing macros involves making changes to the code that drives the macro's actions. This can be as simple as updating a reference to a specific cell, or as complex as adding new functionality with additional code. When editing macros, it is important to take a structured approach to ensure that the macro remains effective and efficient. One best practice is to make changes incrementally, testing each change before moving on to the next. This allows errors to be caught early and ensures that the macro remains functional throughout the editing process.

Adding Buttons to Macros

Adding a button to execute a macro is a convenient way to make the macro easily accessible within the workbook. Buttons can be added to the ribbon, the Quick Access Toolbar, or directly within the worksheet. To add a button to the ribbon or Quick Access Toolbar, go to the Excel Options menu and select Customize Ribbon or Quick Access. From there, you can select the macro in the dropdown list and add it to the desired location. To add a button directly within the worksheet, select the Developer tab and select Insert, then choose the button shape. Assign your macro to the button by right-clicking on it and selecting Assign Macro.

Managing Macro Code

As macros become more complex, the code can become difficult to manage. This can be mitigated by following best practices for code organization. One best practice is to use comments to explain the purpose of each section of code and to make the code easier to understand. Logical groupings of code can also be enclosed in subroutines or functions to make them easier to manage and reuse. Another best practice is to keep the code concise and efficient by minimizing redundancy and using built-in Excel functions where appropriate. This helps reduce the risk of errors and ensures that the macro runs as efficiently as possible.

EDITING MACROS

Editing macros can be a great way to customize your Excel experience to fit your specific needs. Once you have recorded or written a macro, you can change the code to suit your requirements. This subchapter will explore how to edit macros in detail. To edit a macro, first, you need to enable the Developer tab. Go to the File tab, click on Options, choose Customize Ribbon, and then check the Developer box. Once the Developer tab appears in the ribbon, you can navigate to the Macros section and choose the specific macro you want to edit. The Visual Basic Editor (VBE) will open where you can make changes to the macro's code. You can make simple changes such as adding or deleting lines of code, or you can make more complex changes such as adding loops or conditions. It is crucial to test the edited macro thoroughly to ensure that it performs as expected. Make sure to test all possible scenarios and boundaries to guarantee that there are no bugs or errors in the code. It is a good practice to keep a copy of the original macro before making any edits. This way, you have a backup in case something goes wrong. In conclusion, editing macros is a great way to customize and optimize your Excel experience. With the help of VBE and proper testing, you can make changes to code without harming the original code's functionality.Subchapter 3.2: Adding Buttons to Macros Adding buttons to your macros can make it much easier for users to access and run them. Buttons can be added to the Excel ribbon, the Quick Access Toolbar, or directly to the worksheet. To add a macro button to the ribbon, follow these steps: 1. Open the Excel workbook containing the macro you want to use. 2. Click on the File tab, then choose Options. 3. Click on Customize Ribbon in the left-hand pane. 4. In the right-hand pane, select the tab and group where you want to place the macro button. 5. Click on the New Group button to create a new group, if necessary. 6. Select the command that will run your macro from the left-hand pane. 7. Click the Add button to add the command to the selected group. 8. Click OK to close the Excel Options dialog. To add a macro button to the Quick Access Toolbar, follow these steps: 1. Right-click on the Quick Access Toolbar. 2. Choose Customize Quick Access Toolbar. 3. In the left-hand pane, select Macros. 4. Select the macro you want to use. 5. Click the Add button to add the macro to the Quick Access Toolbar. 6. Click OK to close the Excel Options dialog. To add a macro button directly to the worksheet, follow these steps: 1. Open the worksheet where you want to add the button. 2. Click on the Developer tab in the Excel ribbon. 3. Click on Insert, then choose the Button control. 4. Click and drag the mouse to draw the button on the worksheet. 5. In the Assign Macro dialog box, choose the macro you want to run. 6. Enter a name for the button, if desired. 7. Click OK to close the dialog box. Adding buttons to your macros can make them much more accessible for users who are not familiar with Excel or macros. By placing buttons in easy-to-find locations, you can help ensure that your macros are used effectively and efficiently.

SUBCHAPTER 3.3: MANAGING MACRO CODE

Managing macro code is an essential part of maintaining a functional and efficient macro. When dealing with complex macros, it can be challenging to keep track of all the lines of code and their functions. That's why employing good code management practices can make a big difference in the long run. One of the first things you can do is to modularize your macro code. Breaking the code into smaller subroutines or functions can make it more manageable and easier to work with. This also allows you to reuse code in different macros and reduce code duplication. Another good practice is to add comments to your code. Comments are lines of text that are not executed by the macro and are used to explain the purpose or behavior of specific sections of code. This makes it easier for other users to read and understand the macro code, especially if they are unfamiliar with the programming language used. You can also use proper naming conventions for variables, subroutines and functions. This makes the code more understandable and helps you keep track of what each section of code does. For example, instead of naming all variables "var1", "var2", and so on, use descriptive names that convey what the variable is used for, such as "TotalSales", "ShippingCosts", and "CustomerLastName". Finally, don't forget to back up your macro code regularly. Saving multiple copies of your macro code in different locations can help you recover it in case the original code becomes corrupted or lost. Additionally, you can use version control software to track changes made to your macro code over time. By employing good code management practices, you can make your macros easier to work with and maintain in the long run.

Chapter 4: Advanced Macro Techniques

SUBCHAPTER 4.1: LOOPS AND CONDITIONS IN MACROS

Loops and conditions are essential for creating robust and efficient macros. With loops, you can automate repetitive tasks by running a set of instructions multiple times. Variables can be incorporated in loops to repeat an action a specific number of times or until a condition is met. For example, you could create a loop to iterate through a list of sales data and calculate the total revenue. Conditions can be used to make decisions within a macro. For instance, you may want to check whether a specific condition is true before proceeding with a task. This could be useful, for example, if you want to automatically copy and paste data from one sheet to another, but only if the data meets certain criteria.

For Loops

One common type of loop is a "For loop," which can loop through a set of values a specified number of times. This can be useful for performing calculations or formatting data in tables. Here's an example of a basic For loop that counts from 1 to 10:
``` For i = 1 To 10 ' Do something Next i ```

If Statements

If statements are used to perform different actions depending on whether a certain condition is true or false. For example, you might want to check whether a certain cell contains a specific value before proceeding with a macro. Here is an example of an If statement: ``` If Range("A1").Value = "Yes" Then ' Do something if A1 equals "Yes" Else ' Do something else if A1 does not equal "Yes" End If ```
```

SUBCHAPTER 4.2: ERROR HANDLING IN MACROS

No matter how carefully you design your macros, errors can sometimes occur. Error handling is the process of anticipating and preventing errors within a macro. By taking steps to handle errors, you can prevent your macro from crashing or providing incorrect results. One approach to error handling is to use "On Error" statements, which allow you to specify how Excel should react when an error is encountered during macro execution. For example, you might use an On Error statement to display a message to the user if an error occurs. Another approach is to validate user input at the beginning of the macro to ensure that it meets certain criteria. This can prevent errors from occurring further down the line.

SUBCHAPTER 4.3:
INTERACTING WITH OTHER APPLICATIONS

Excel macros can interact with other applications on your computer to further automate your workflow. For example, you might use a macro to automate the process of entering data into an external database or publishing data to a website. To interact with a specific application, you will typically need to include information about the application's object model in your macro. This might involve creating an instance of the application or calling particular functions within the application's API. For example, to interact with Microsoft Word, you might use a syntax like the following: ``` Set WordApp = CreateObject("Word.Application")
WordApp.Documents.Add
WordApp.Visible = True ``` This code would open a new instance of Microsoft Word, create a new document, and set the

document to be visible. By combining Excel macros with other applications, you can create powerful automation that can save you a significant amount of time and effort.

LOOPS AND CONDITIONS IN MACROS

Loops and conditions can significantly enhance the functionality of macros. Loops allow your macro to repeat a set of instructions multiple times, while conditions enable your macro to make decisions based on certain criteria. The combination of loops and conditions can produce powerful and effective macros that can automate complex tasks within Excel.

For Loops

For loops are one of the most common types of loops used in macros. They allow the macro to execute a set of instructions a specific number of times. For example, you could use a for loop to iterate through the rows in a table and perform a specific calculation on each row. Here is an example of a for loop that iterates through the cells in a specified range: ```VB For Each cell In Range("A1:A10") 'Do something with the cell Next cell ```

Do Loops

Do loops are another type of loop that can be used in macros. They allow the macro to execute a set of instructions repeatedly until a certain condition is met. For example, you could use a do loop to repeatedly prompt the user for input until a valid value is entered. Here is an example of a do loop that prompts the user for input until a valid value is entered: ```VB Do InputValue = InputBox("Please enter a value between 1 and 10", "Input Value") Loop Until InputValue >= 1 And InputValue <= 10 ```

If Statements

If statements are a type of condition that can be used in macros. They allow the macro to make decisions based on certain criteria. For example, you could use an if statement to determine if a certain cell contains a specific value. Here is an example of an if statement that checks if a cell contains the value "Yes": ```VB If Range("A1").Value = "Yes" Then 'Do something if the cell contains "Yes" End If```

Select Case Statements

Select case statements are another type of condition that can be used in macros. They allow the macro to select a specific set of instructions based on the value of a variable or expression. For example, you could use a select case statement to handle different input values. Here is an example of a select case statement that handles different input values: ```VB Select Case InputValue Case 1 'Do something if InputValue equals 1 Case 2 'Do something if InputValue equals 2 Case Else 'Do something if InputValue is not 1 or 2 End Select ```

Combining Loops and Conditions

Loops and conditions can also be combined in macros to create more complex functionality. For example, you could use a for loop to iterate through a range of cells and use an if statement to check if each cell contains a certain value. Here is an example of a for loop that iterates through a range of cells and uses an if statement to check if each cell contains the value "Yes": ```VB For Each cell In Range("A1:A10") If cell.Value = "Yes" Then 'Do something if the cell contains "Yes" End If Next cell ``` By utilizing loops and conditions in your macros, you can make them more efficient and effective in automating tasks within Excel.

SUBCHAPTER 4.2: ERROR HANDLING IN MACROS

Error handling is an important aspect of macro programming. It is essential to handle errors gracefully in your macros to avoid unexpected results that can cause data loss or program crashes. In this subchapter, we will discuss the best practices for handling errors in macros. One common approach to error handling in VBA macros is the use of **On Error** statements. This approach involves placing one or more On Error statements at the beginning of each code section that could potentially raise an error. These statements allow you to specify what to do when an error occurs, such as displaying an error message, undoing the last action, or exiting the macro. The On Error statement can be used in three modes: **On Error GoTo 0**, **On Error Resume Next**, and **On Error GoTo label**. The **On Error GoTo 0** mode disables error handling, meaning that the macro will halt and display error messages if an error occurs. This mode is useful during the initial development phase of your macro, but it is risky to leave it active during the final testing phase. The **On Error Resume Next** mode tells the macro to ignore any errors and continue with the next line of code. This approach is useful for situations where an error is expected, such as when deleting a file that may or may not exist. The **On Error GoTo label** mode allows you to define a label (a marker in the code) that the macro will jump to if an error occurs. This mode allows you to handle the error gracefully by displaying a custom error message, undoing the last action, or exiting the macro. In addition to On Error statements, you can also use **Try...Catch** blocks to handle specific exceptions in your macro code. A try block can contain one or more catch blocks that catch specific exceptions and handle them appropriately. To summarize, error handling is a critical aspect of macro programming that can help avoid unexpected results or program crashes. By using On Error statements and Try...Catch blocks, you can handle errors gracefully and make your macros more robust and reliable.

INTERACTING WITH OTHER APPLICATIONS

Excel Macros are not limited to Excel alone. It can interact and communicate with other applications, allowing you to automate more complex tasks that involve other software. You can, for example, use your Excel Macros to extract data from different databases and applications, perform calculations on it, and then use the results to generate reports in other applications. One example of interacting with other applications is automating the sending of emails. With a Macro, you can automatically generate and send emails from Excel based on specific criteria or conditions. This can save you time and reduce errors that may occur if sending emails manually. Another example is using your Macro to open and control other applications. You might use a Macro to launch Microsoft Word, for example, and perform formatting or other tasks automatically. Or you might use a Macro to communicate with a web application, extract data, and then use it in your Excel spreadsheet. Overall, the ability for Excel Macros to interact with other applications significantly improves the potential for workflow automation, allowing you to accomplish more complex and time-consuming tasks with ease.

Chapter 5: Macros for Data Analysis

With the increasing amount of data, businesses need automated ways to analyze and process data efficiently. Excel macros are a great solution for time-consuming and repetitive data analysis tasks. This chapter is dedicated to exploring different techniques for automating data analysis with Macros.

SUBCHAPTER 5.1: SORTING AND FILTERING DATA WITH MACROS

Sorting and filtering are essential techniques for data analysis that help in identifying the relevant data subset from a large dataset. Excel macros can automate the sorting and filtering process of data tables, making it quicker and easier. With macros, users can create a custom sorting and filtering formula, including sorting by multiple columns, sorting by colors, filtering by text, and more. This automation process saves time and provides accurate results by eliminating manual errors.

Subchapter 5.1.1: Automating Sorting with Macros

Excel macros can be used to automate sorting that saves time and ensures accurate results. For instance, a macro can be created to sort data based on a specific column in ascending order or descending order. By doing so, users can get a clear view of the dataset without sorting the data manually.

Subchapter 5.1.2: Automating Filtering with Macros

Filters are a subset of data that meets specific criteria, and Excel macros can automate filters to make it quicker and easier. As an example, macros can be set up to automatically filter data based on a particular column or range of columns. Users can apply a range of filters based on text, color, numbers, and dates to get quick insights from their data.

SUBCHAPTER 5.2: PIVOTTABLES AUTOMATION

PivotTables are an excellent feature in Excel to simplify complex data into easily digestible formats. Macros can be used to automate the generation of PivotTables with a single click saving time and effort. Users can customize their PivotTables to display relevant data and insights from complex datasets and export reports or charts automatically.

Subchapter 5.2.1: Creating PivotTables with Macros

With Excel macros, users can create PivotTables with customizations on data ranges, rows, columns, and more. PivotTables with custom formulas can also be created with macros to provide better insights into datasets. Users can predefine styles and formatting for PivotTables formation defined by their organization or team.

Subchapter 5.2.2: Exporting Reports and Charts from PivotTables

Exporting reports and charts from PivotTables are an essential requirement for many organizations. And this process can be streamlined with the use of Excel Macros. By setting up Macros to automate the report export process, reports can be created in specific formats and shared in seconds, saving time and effort.

SUBCHAPTER 5.3: CHARTS AND DASHBOARDS WITH MACROS

For businesses, creating and maintaining Dashboards and Charts is crucial for data-driven decision-making. Excel macros can automate the creation of charts and dashboards with easily readable data. This automation process can help in data visualization and analysis and report generation.

Subchapter 5.3.1: Automating Charts and Graphs Creation with Macros

Excel macros can be customized to create and populate charts with selected data areas automatically. This automated process can allow the creation of charts, including line charts, bar charts, and pie charts, through Macros. By automating the charts and graphs creation process, users can save time and can easily and repeatedly create charts and graphs that are consistent and relevant to their business use case.

Subchapter 5.3.2: Dashboard Automation with Macros

Excel Macros can be a game-changer when it comes to automating dashboard creation. Without an effective automation tool, creating charts and dashboards can be a time-consuming task. Macros allow users to automate dashboard creation, including chart creation, chart formatting, and populating data into the dashboard. By removing the time-consuming and repetitive tasks of dashboard and chart creation, users can create dashboards that provide relevant insights to decision-makers.

SORTING AND FILTERING DATA WITH MACROS

When working with large sets of data in Excel, it is essential to sort and filter the data efficiently. Sorting organizes the data in a specific order, while filtering limits the data that is visible based on specific criteria. With macros, sorting and filtering can be automated, saving you considerable time and effort. To sort data using macros, you need to specify the sorting order and the range of cells to sort. You can sort based on a single column or multiple columns, with each column having its own sorting order. You can also customize the sorting criteria by specifying if the data should be sorted in ascending or descending order. Filtering data can be done in several ways. You can filter by a specific value within a column, use a custom filter to display data that meets specific conditions, or use multiple criteria to filter the data. With macro-enabled worksheets, all these filters can be automated. Creating such macros requires an understanding of VBA and its basic syntax. You can record a macro to apply a sort or filter, but editing the code directly provides more robust customization options. In conclusion, sorting and filtering data can be done much more efficiently with macros. With macros, you can sort data in specific orders based on multiple criteria and quickly filter data based on certain conditions. Knowing how to use these tools proficiently will enable you to handle large sets of data with ease.**PivotTables Automation** PivotTables are a powerful tool in Excel that allow you to analyze and summarize large amounts of data. With the help of macros, you can automate the creation and management of PivotTables, saving you time and effort. To create a PivotTable using a macro, you first need to record the steps involved in creating the PivotTable. This includes selecting the data range, choosing the rows and columns to use, and specifying any filters or calculations to apply. Once you have recorded the PivotTable creation steps, you can then modify and customize the macro code to suit your specific needs. This may include adding more advanced calculations or formatting options, or automating the refresh or update of the PivotTable based on changes to the underlying data. With PivotTable automation, you can quickly create and manipulate complex datasets, gaining valuable insights and reducing the risk of errors or inaccuracies. So why not give it a try in your next data analysis project?Subchapter 5.3: Charts and Dashboards with Macros Charts and dashboards are powerful tools for analyzing and presenting data. With Excel macros, you can automate the creation and updating of charts and dashboards to save time and increase accuracy. First, let's talk about creating charts with macros. You can record a macro to create a chart from scratch or modify an existing chart. When recording a macro, make sure to select the appropriate data range and chart type. You can also customize the chart's design and layout to fit your needs. Once you have created a chart, you can use macros to update it with new data. For example, you can record a macro to add new rows or columns of data to a chart's source range. You can also use macros to change the chart's title, axis labels, and other chart elements. Dashboards are collections of charts, tables, and other visualizations that provide a high-level overview of data. With Excel macros, you can automate the creation and updating of dashboards to keep stakeholders informed and up-to-date. To create a dashboard with macros, start by selecting the data ranges for each chart or table. You can then record macros to create each visual element of the dashboard. For example, you can record a macro to create a line chart that shows sales over time, and another macro to create a table that shows the top-selling products. With your macros recorded, you can run them all at once to create the complete dashboard. You can also use macros to update the dashboard with new data. For example, you can record a macro to add a new row of data to a table or update a chart's source range. In conclusion, automating the creation and updating of charts and dashboards with macros can help you save time and increase the accuracy of your data analysis. With practice, you can become proficient at using macros to create professional-looking charts and dashboards that will impress stakeholders and drive business decisions.

Chapter 6: Macros and Collaboration

SUBCHAPTER 6.1: MANAGING SHARED WORKBOOKS WITH MACROS

Collaboration is a critical component of modern workplaces. Often, multiple employees may need to work on the same workbook at the same time. Excel has the option to work on a workbook collaboratively using the "Shared

Workbook" feature. When a workbook is shared, multiple users can edit it at the same time, and their changes are automatically saved. However, the shared workbook feature has some limitations when it comes to using macros. Macros cannot be recorded or run when the workbook is shared. Therefore, it is essential to know how to manage shared workbooks when using macros. To manage shared workbooks with macros, you need to follow specific guidelines. First, avoid creating a new macro or editing an existing one when someone else is using the shared workbook. This can cause errors and conflicts. When creating a macro, make sure it won't conflict with other users' actions. For example, if a macro is designed to insert new rows into a table, make sure it will not insert rows above other users' data who are editing the sheet at the same time. Finally, ensure to test macros thoroughly before sharing them. In a shared workbook, even a simple mistake or an error in your macro code can cause problems for everyone.

SUBCHAPTER 6.2: USING MACROS FOR DATA CONSOLIDATION

Data consolidation is a frequent task in the workplace where several sources of data need to be combined into a single, usable format. Excel offers various tools for data consolidation but using macros can be an efficient way of automating the process. A macro can help consolidate data from multiple workbooks or worksheets into a single location. It can also apply formatting and calculations to the consolidated data making it easier to work with. To create a macro for data consolidation, start by defining the data sources. Then, write a code that will extract the data from each source and place it into a new worksheet or workbook. Before running the macro, consider exceptions, such as incomplete data or duplicates. The macro can perform quality checks before consolidation, such as checking for missing data points or highlighting duplicate entries.

SUBCHAPTER 6.3: SHARING LIBRARIES OF MACROS AND ADD-INS

Using macros and add-ins can help streamline tasks and automate repetitive processes for multiple employees. Sharing libraries of macros and add-ins can save time and improve efficiency in the workplace. Excel offers two ways to share macros and add-ins: Personal Macro Workbook and Shared Add-ins. The Personal Macro Workbook allows users to save macros that are available in all workbooks opened by the same user. In contrast, Shared Add-ins are available for all users on a given machine. To share a macro library, start by creating a new workbook and recording your macro(s). Then save the workbook as an Excel Add-In. This is done by changing the file extension to "xlam." For shared add-ins, the add-in file needs to be stored in a location that is accessible to all users of the machine. To ensure that the add-in loads automatically every time Excel is opened, save the add-in in the Excel Add-ins folder. Remember to test the macros and add-ins thoroughly before sharing them. A small mistake can cause errors for all users who access them. Consider providing training or documentation on how to use the macro libraries to ensure seamless adoption.

MANAGING SHARED WORKBOOKS WITH MACROS

Sharing workbooks can save time and effort by allowing multiple people to collaborate on a single document. However, it can be difficult to manage changes and updates from multiple users. This is where macros can be especially helpful. One way to manage shared workbooks with macros is by automating the tracking and merging of changes. You can create a macro that will track changes made by each user and automatically merge them into a single document. This can help streamline the process and ensure that all changes are properly accounted for. Another useful macro feature for shared workbooks is the ability to restrict access to certain areas of the document. This can help prevent accidental changes or deletions from other users. By setting up these restrictions with macros, you can easily enable or disable access for certain users or groups. Lastly, you can use macros to create customized forms that allow for data input and collaboration between multiple users. These forms can be designed to fit the specific needs of your project and can help simplify the process of collecting and organizing data from multiple sources. Overall, macros offer a powerful tool for managing shared workbooks in a way that is efficient, effective, and customizable to your specific needs.

USING MACROS FOR DATA CONSOLIDATION

Data consolidation can be a time-consuming task that involves merging data from different sources, removing duplicates, and reconciling inconsistencies. Fortunately, macros can simplify this process and enable users to consolidate data with just a few clicks. One popular approach for consolidating data is to use the VLOOKUP function, which allows you to search for a value in one table and return a corresponding value from another table. Macros can automate this process by looping through multiple tables and performing VLOOKUP functions on each one. This can save users hours of manual labor and ensure that data is accurate and consistent. Another commonly used technique for consolidating data through macros is to create a master worksheet that pulls data from multiple sources. The macro would then loop through each data source and extract the required data to populate the master worksheet. This technique is particularly useful when dealing with large data sets or when working with data from external sources. Users can also leverage macros to clean and standardize data during the consolidation process. For example, macros can be used to remove duplicates, transpose data, or convert data types. This can enhance the accuracy and usability of consolidated data and make it easier to analyze and visualize. In addition to saving time, macros can also improve the accuracy and consistency of consolidated data by minimizing the risk of human error. With macros, users can easily repeat and modify the consolidation process as needed and ensure that data is up-to-date and reliable. Overall, using macros for data consolidation is an effective way to streamline and simplify this critical business process. By automating repetitive tasks and standardizing data, macros can enhance productivity, accuracy, and decision-making.

SHARING LIBRARIES OF MACROS AND ADD-INS

Are you tired of recreating the same macros over and over again for each new workbook? Do you want to save time and increase efficiency by sharing your macros and add-ins with others? Look no further than sharing libraries of macros and add-ins! Sharing libraries of macros and add-ins allows you to consolidate all of your commonly used macros and functions into a single location. This can then be shared with other users, allowing them to easily access the same macros and functions without having to recreate them from scratch. Creating a shared library is easy, simply save your commonly used macros and add-ins into a separate workbook or add-in file. Once this is done, the file can then be shared with others through a shared drive or email. The recipient can then install or save the file, allowing them to access the macros and add-ins directly from their own workbooks.

Not only does sharing libraries of macros and add-ins save time and increase efficiency, it also ensures consistency across all workbooks. This can be particularly useful for businesses or organizations with multiple employees working on similar projects, ensuring that everyone is using the same macros and functions. In conclusion, sharing libraries of macros and add-ins is a powerful tool that can save time and increase efficiency for individuals and businesses alike. By consolidating your commonly used macros and functions into a single location, you can ensure consistency and streamline your workflow. Give it a try today and see how it can benefit you!

Conclusion and Resources

Congratulations! You have made it through the entire book, "Efficient Workflow with Excel Macros." In this book, we covered a variety of topics to help you improve your workflow efficiency with Excel Macros. In Chapter 1, we started with an overview of macros and their benefits. We also covered macro security to help you protect your files from malicious or undesired macro code. Chapter 2 focused on recording macros, including steps to record a macro, editing and debugging macros, and best practices for creating macros. In Chapter 3, we discussed how to modify macros by editing, adding buttons, and managing macro code. Chapter 4 delved into advanced macro techniques such as loops and conditions, error handling, and interacting with other applications. Chapter 5 covered macros for data analysis, including sorting and filtering data, pivot tables automation, and charts and dashboards. In Chapter 6, we discussed how macros can help with collaboration by managing shared workbooks, data consolidation, and sharing libraries of macros and add-ins. In this final chapter, we recap the key points of each chapter, provide further training and resources, and include a glossary of terms to help you better understand macro-related terminology. Overall, we hope this book has been informative and useful in improving your efficiency with Excel Macros. We encourage you to continue learning and exploring this powerful tool to enhance your workflow. To further your knowledge, we recommend checking out online forums and communities, attending workshops and training sessions, and exploring online courses and tutorials. Additionally, Microsoft provides extensive documentation and support for Excel Macros on their website. Thank you for reading "Efficient Workflow with Excel Macros." We hope you found it helpful and wish you the best on your macro-driven journey towards increased efficiency.Subchapter 7.1: Recap of Key Points Throughout this book, we have covered a multitude of topics related to Excel Macros and their benefits for efficient workflow. Let's take a moment to review some of the key points from each chapter: Chapter 1: Understanding Macros - Macros are a set of recorded actions that automate repetitive tasks in Excel. - The benefits of using Macros include time-saving, efficiency, and accuracy. - Macro security is an important consideration to prevent malicious code from harming your computer. Chapter 2: Recording Macros - Steps to record a Macro include enabling the Developer tab, selecting a worksheet, and recording actions. - Editing and debugging Macros allows you to modify and correct errors in your Macro code. - It is important to follow best practices for creating Macros, such as naming conventions and descriptive comments. Chapter 3: Modifying Macros - Editing Macros involves changing the recorded actions, while adding buttons to Macros can create a user-friendly interface. - Managing Macro code allows you to organize and optimize your code for better efficiency. Chapter 4: Advanced Macro Techniques - Loops and conditions are powerful tools for creating dynamic Macros that can handle complex tasks. - Error handling in Macros can help prevent crashes and address potential errors. - Interacting with other applications expands the possibilities of what you can accomplish with Macros. Chapter 5: Macros for Data Analysis - Sorting and filtering data with Macros can save time and effort in data analysis. - PivotTables automation streamlines the creation and updating of PivotTables. - Charts and dashboards with Macros allow for interactive and dynamic data visualization. Chapter 6: Macros and Collaboration - Managing shared workbooks with Macros helps keep multiple users organized and on the same page. - Using Macros for data consolidation can simplify the process of combining data from multiple sources. - Sharing libraries of Macros and add-ins can increase efficiency for you and your team. In conclusion, Excel Macros can be an indispensable tool for anyone looking to increase productivity and efficiency in their Excel workflow. By following best practices and utilizing advanced techniques, you can create powerful Macros that save time and effort. Remember to always consider security and collaborate with your team to make the most of your Macro capabilities.

FURTHER TRAINING AND RESOURCES

Learning Excel Macros can be an exciting journey towards streamlining your workflow and increasing productivity. If you are eager to learn more about Macros, here are some further training and resources that can help you improve.

Online Tutorials

There are countless online tutorials available that can help you master Excel Macros. Websites like Udemy, Coursera, and LinkedIn Learning offer comprehensive courses that can take you from beginner to expert level.

Excel Community

Joining an Excel community can be a great way to grow and learn from other experts in the field. Online forums like r/excel offer a platform where you can interact with professionals and get answers to your Macro-related questions, share ideas, and learn new tricks.

Excel Books and Blogs

Another way to expand your knowledge and get a deeper understanding of Excel Macros is by reading books and blogs. Platforms like Amazon offer a wide range of books on Excel Macros from beginner to advanced level. You can also find excellent blogs such as Excel Campus, Excel Champs, and Excel Easy, which offer useful tips and tricks for working with macros.

Excel MVPs

Excel Most Valuable Professionals (MVPs) are experts who volunteer their time to help other users understand the ins and outs of Excel Macros. These experts are knowledgeable and experienced, and they can provide valuable insights to help you improve your Macros skills. You can find Excel MVPs on social media platforms like Twitter and LinkedIn. In conclusion, there are many resources available online that can help you learn and master Excel Macros. By investing the time to explore these resources, you can set yourself up for success and become a Macros pro in no time.

www.ingramcontent.com/pod-product-compliance
Lightning Source LLC
Chambersburg PA
CBHW070820220526

45466CB00002B/727